Poetry & Art

by

Howard Hendrickson

Featuring paintings by

Brenda Hendrickson

Woodpecker Press, LLC
Livingston, NJ

Poetry & Art

Published by

Woodpecker Press, LLC

www.WoodpeckerPress.com

ISBN: 978-1-937397-48-7 (sc)

ISBN: 978-1-937397-49-4 (epub)

Printed in the United States of America

Cover Design: Nu-Image Design, www.nu-imagedesign.com

Paintings: Brenda Hendrickson, www.brendahendricksonfineart.com

Dedication

To all who appreciate fine art and to those who enjoy reading poetry

To those who inspired me to write poems based on your suggestions and special requests

To those who influenced me, namely, my creative writing and English literature instructors

To Brenda, for gracing the Art & Poetry section of my book with her beautiful abstract paintings, which inspired my poems

ACKNOWLEDGMENTS

From Howard Hendrickson

First and foremost, I am grateful to my wife, Brenda, for her support through the years. Her input and critiquing of my poems were invaluable to the finished product.

My thanks go to Anthony Fiore for the honor of including my poem "The Golfer" in his photo golfing book, *Wicked's World of Golf* (Blurb Books, 2011). This allowed me to gain the exposure outside the world of poetry.

Lastly, thank you to Rosanna Imbriano, who asked me to write a poem for her father's funeral. It was a challenge, but the results were very much appreciated by her. She gave me the privilege of reading my poem at the Sempre Avanti 5th Anniversary Gala, held in Cedar Grove, New Jersey. Rosanna is the founder and executive director of Sempre Avanti, Inc., a 501(c)(3) nonprofit.

These experiences have given me the opportunity for other poetry readings and other writing assignments.

Thank you, Dan Yeager of Nu-Image Design, for the cover design. Your artistic artistry is unsurpassed. Thank you, Donna Thompson of Woodpecker Press. Your editing, proofreading, and publishing insight were essential. It was a pleasure working with both of you again.

From Brenda Hendrickson

I thank everyone who supported me by attending my art shows and exhibits. I am also appreciative to the members of the West Essex Art Association for the many opportunities to exhibit at the Koelher Art Gallery at Crane's Mill.

I am particularly grateful for the opportunity to hold my one-woman art shows at the Pine Brook and Montville branches of Kearny Bank and at the Parsippany Library. These events encouraged me to continue with my abstract painting.

And, of course, I thank Howard for allowing me to share the pages of this book with my paintings and for the beautiful poems they inspired him to write.

Thanks go out to all those who, though the years, have supported and encouraged our individual endeavors.

Table of Contents

Family & Social

WELCOME TO OUR HOUSE

Welcome to our house, won't you come on in?
Pull up a chair and let the fun begin.
We're so glad to have you here,
Open up the fridge and grab yourself a beer.
Soon I'll be lighting up the grill,
Then we'll eat until we have our fill.
It's always great when good friends get together
The good times never end regardless of the weather.
Later around the fire pit, we'll make a lot of s'mores.
There are plenty, so don't be afraid to ask for more.
Someone brings out a guitar and we all start to sing.
Oh, what happiness a little song can bring!
Alas! The hour is now getting late
Seeing you all has been really great.
We hope you enjoyed the time we had to spend
We can't wait until you come back again.

IN PRAISE OF COFFEE

Whether the coffee is drip or perk,
I need a cup before I go to work.
Either medium or dark roast,
I have some with my eggs and toast.

Cappuccino, mocha, or latte,
What better way to start the day?
In a mug or in a cup,
Just pour it in and I'll drink it up.

Espresso or café au lait,
I like my coffee almost any way.
Whether whole bean or fine grind,
Coffee helps me to unwind.

At my favorite coffee shop,
I drink until the very last drop.
I like my coffee piping hot.
If I could, I'd drink the whole pot.

Pour me some coffee (please no decaf),
Add some milk or half and half.
If it's bitter some sugar will make it sweet.
A good cup of coffee is hard to beat.

KARAOKE NIGHT

It's karaoke night down at Stewart Hall.
All the local folks are there, they always have a ball.
There's a list of all the songs laying on a table,
Pick the one you'd like to sing whenever you are able.
There are hundreds that you can choose.
So, pick one out. What have you got to lose?
You don't have to know an A sharp from B flat,
Just read the words on the screen and have a go at that.
Go ahead and sing a song, sing it loud and strong.
No matter how well you sing, you cannot go wrong.
Even if you're out of tune or cannot keep a beat,
Just being with your friends, will make the night complete.
So, go on up and give it a try. For when all is said and done,
You'll be glad you did, because it was a lot of fun.

BOWLING TIPS

If you want the ball to go straight and true,
Here are some things that you must do.
Find the proper weight if you can,
Make sure you have the right finger span.
Then you need a comfortable stance,
And count your steps, don't try to dance.
Aim for the pocket (pins one and two).
Keep your wrist straight and follow through.
Try to get the perfect spin,
So you can knock down all ten pins.
If you have three strikes in a row,
That's called a turkey as you know.
But if you get an open frame,
You only have yourself to blame.
I'd hate to see you go in the gutter,
That would surely make me shutter.
If you get a spare in every frame,
You will have a really good game.

THE OLD WROUGHT IRON GATE

Last night while on a walk, I passed an old wrought iron gate.
It was a beautiful work of art I never knew was there.
I thought, "I must not linger," as the hour was getting late.
But still I stood and began to stare
At the old wrought iron gate.

I wondered what was hidden behind old wrought iron gate,
But I could not see no matter how I tried.
I also wondered what would be my fate,
If somehow I could be on the other side
Of the old wrought iron gate.

As I gazed upon the old wrought iron gate,
My imagination began to grow.
I thought, "It would be so great
If somehow I could go
And venture past the old wrought iron gate.

But as I approached the old wrought iron gate,
My hopes began to disappear because the gate was locked.
Perhaps I'll come back again at some later date.
Maybe once inside I may well be shocked
To find what lies behind the old wrought iron gate.

As I walked away from the old wrought iron gate,
In the distance I heard an eerie shrill.
So, I quickly decided to increase my gait.
My walk turned into a run as my blood began to chill.
I just had to get far away from the old wrought iron gate.

THE CHANGE OF SEASONS

Some folks like a climate that's sunny all the time
To them if it rains or snows, it would be a crime.
If that makes them happy, I guess they have their reasons
But as for me, I like the change of seasons.

The year begins in winter, when the ground is covered white.
With all the falling snow, it's such a pretty sight.
The temperature is cold both day and night,
But you'll be warm if you hold your loved one tight.

The vernal equinox marks the start of spring,
When flowers begin to bud and birds begin to sing.
Leaves and grass are turning green thanks to gentle rain.
Nights are shorter and days grow longer once again.

Summer days are long and hot due to blazing sun,
So, we head out to the beach to have some water fun.
Picnics and barbeques are a special treat.
Yes, summer is a time of year that's really hard to beat.

Then along comes autumn, my favorite time of all,
When frost is on the pumpkin and leaves begin to fall.
The nights start getting cooler and a nip is in the air,
But I wear a nice warm sweater, so I don't really care.

Some folks like the weather warm for their own reasons.
Others prefer it on the cooler side.
However, I enjoy the change of seasons,
A fact I cannot hide.

BARE WALLS

Sitting in my living room looking at the walls,
It isn't right that all of them are bare.
I must rectify the situation
By hanging some pictures there.

Perhaps above the fireplace
I'll hang a landscape scene,
One with clouds of white, a sky of blue
And trees of evergreen.

Maybe over the couch
Would be the perfect place
To put the ballet dancer
So I can enjoy her grace.

A still life near the table
Would make me stare for hours
As I sit admiring
All the fruit and flowers.

By the window I think I'll place
An abstract painting
With geometric shapes
That should match perfectly
With the rug and drapes.

Finally, at the door
Hanging high above
I'll place for all to see
A portrait of my love
Smiling down on me.

HOORAY, IT'S THE WEEKEND

After working hard all week, the weekend is finally here.
I think I'll just relax and have a nice cold beer.
Tomorrow I'll work around the yard,
Mow the grass and weed, but I won't work too hard.
Later, I'll put some steaks on the grill
My wife and I will eat til we've had our fill.
I like mine well done; she likes medium rare.
Anyway, a good steak is beyond compare.
Maybe afterward, we'll go for a walk
Or perhaps just sit around and talk.
Take some time just for the two of us
Without any unnecessary noise or fuss.
Next comes Sunday, a day of rest
When we give thanks that we've been blessed.
With good health and the love we share
We've got friends and family everywhere.
The weekend has come to an end
And, Monday it's back to work again.

THE POOL LESSON

I stopped at my local pub one day
And saw an empty pool table.
So I asked, "Would anyone like to play?
I'm ready if you're able."
Someone said, "I'd like to challenge you,"
Then he took out his custom-made cue.
"Let's see if you have what it takes,
Go ahead, my friend, you can break."
I sank two balls to start the match,
But then I proceeded to scratch.
This gave him a chance to cause me woe,
As he sank seven balls in a row.
With one more shot to seal my fate,
He easily sank the eight.
I learned my lesson very quick,
Never play with someone who has his own cue stick.

THE POTLUCK DINNER

We get together every Friday night
For a potluck dinner that's a real delight.
You never know what you may get
Each week it gets better yet.
Chicken wings and assorted greens
Or maybe fried rice or pork and beans.
It could be pasta or mac and cheese
Maybe a mix of carrots and peas.
There could even be garlic bread,
So everyone is always well fed.
Meatballs, both Italian and Swedish style,
Lots of choices to make you smile.
A salad made with spinach and berries,
Homemade cake topped with cherries,
Pork served with sauerkraut,
The food is so good you want to shout.
Someone brought sausage and peppers.
What, no hasenpfeffer?
It's a dish made with cheese and zucchinis.
And, there's a plate of cocktail wienies.
With all the many types of food,
To leave any behind would be just rude.
The potluck dinner is a wonderful treat
Especially when it ends with something sweet.

THE JOYS OF AUTUMN

Another season's over; summer went by so fast.
The days are getting longer; autumn is here at last.
Apples are in the orchard, pumpkins are in the field,
Farmers are harvesting, I wonder what will be the yield.
Leaves on trees are turning red and brown
It's such a pretty sight until they all fall down.
Autumn is exciting with all there is to do,
So much activity before the season's through.
Street fairs and festivals and all the fun they bring,
Along with Halloween filled with scary things.
Then comes Thanksgiving when we give thanks and pray
For all the blessings that we enjoy each day.
So let's enjoy the Autumn because before you know,
Winter will be upon us and we'll have to deal with snow.

THE HANDYMAN

I'm a handyman, I'll take any job I can.
Just give me a call, 'cause I'm your man.
If you want a nice clean room,
I have my own mop and broom.
I can mow the grass and cut the weeds.
If you want a garden, I can plant some seeds.
I can clean your gutters, make them look like new.
There's not a job that I can't do.
I can paint your house both inside and out.
If your hose faucet leaks, I can change the spout.
I can trim the hedges or trim a tree.
Never hesitate to call on me.
If your window is leaking, I can fix the sash.
And when I'm finished, I'll haul away the trash.
No matter what the job is, I'll work very hard.
But please remember, I don't take credit cards.

A GOOD DAY NO DOUBT

While walking in the park one day
In the merry month of May,
I looked up to the skies
And much to my surprise
A dark cloud was heading my way.

"This is not good," I thought.
"If I don't hurry, in the storm I'll be caught."
But nowhere did I see
Any shelter near to me.
How I wished an umbrella I had brought.

Suddenly up ahead I spied
A place where I could safely hide.
Once the rain started pouring down,
I knew for sure that I could drown.
So, quickly I ran inside.

Now I was inside a diner
Where things could not be finer.
I got myself a little treat
Hot coffee and a bun so sweet.
The waitress couldn't be any finer.

Soon the sun once again came out,
No need now to sit and pout
I paid my check and said, "Goodbye,"
And walked out under a clear blue sky.
It'll be a good day after all, no doubt.

NEIGHBORHOOD BAR

If you want to have some fun, here's where you should go.
Anytime you enter, there's someone you will know.
It's near where you love, so you won't have to travel far,
Just go down to your local neighborhood bar.

Happy hour starts at five and ends at half past nine,
No matter when you get there, you'll have a real good time.
The bartender treats you well, so leave a tip in his jar.
Everyone is so cordial at your local neighborhood bar.

The rocking band plays loud every Friday night.
You know everybody in the crowd, not a stranger is in sight.
Someone will even take you home if you don't have a car.
It's all one big family at your local neighborhood bar.

Some nights it's open mic if you want to sing along
Or maybe just listen if you don't know a song.
But if you like karaoke you could be a star,
'cause everybody loves you at your local neighborhood bar.

JACK'S LAST DERBY DAY

Today is the day we hated to face,
Jack is hosting his last Derby Race.
It started as a backyard barbecue
But through the years it grew and grew.
Soon it was known throughout the town
The party had become renown
People came from far and near
To bet on the horses, eat food, and drink beer.
So, before the horses speed around the track,
Let's all lift our glasses and say, "Thank you, Jack!"

LET'S FORGET

Let's forget about the hate
And concentrate on love.
Let's forget about being hawks
And be more like a dove.
Let's forget about the fear
And learn how to be brave.
Let's forget about pollution
So our planet we can save.
Let's forget about the greed
And learn to share the wealth.
Let's forget about the pain
And concentrate on health
Let's forget about the wars
And try to live in peace.
Maybe if we learn to care
All violence will finally cease.

SAY A LITTLE PRAYER FOR ME

When you go to church on Sunday
And you start to pray
As you go down on your knees
Say a little prayer for me.

If you take a trip around the world
I hope it sets your heart a whirl
As you sail from sea to sea
Say a little prayer for me.

I wish you great success
And I wish you all the best
Become all that you can be
Just say a little prayer for me.

When you travel throughout this land
I know you'll find it's truly grand
Make sure you see all you can see
But say a little prayer for me.

While lying in your bed tonight
With the covers pulled up tight,
As you're resting comfortably
Say a little prayer for me.

COPING WITH COVID-19

I need lotion for my face,
I think I'll buy one whole case.
Everyone knows I'm not a dope,
So I'll get a case of soap.
You know I'm really smart.
I'm filling up the shopping cart.
Forget about my fellow man,
I'm buying everything I can.
I need disinfectant, bleach, hand wipes,
And drain cleaner for my pipes,
Paper towels, tissues, and tp,
I'm buying everything I see.
Floor polish and aerosol spray,
I don't need water but will buy it anyway.
Folks might think I'm being rude,
Since I'm buying all the food.
Twelve cans of tuna and mac & cheese,
Eight jars of tomato sauce if you please,
Chips and dip and soda, too,
Twenty cans of soup and stew,
Five jars of pb & jelly,
Things I need to fill my belly.
Maybe three loaves of bread,
I'm determined to be well-fed.
I think I'll buy two dozen eggs
And some frozen chicken legs.
You may think I bought a lot,
But if there's something I forgot,
The store is open until ten.
I can always come back again.

SIX FEET AWAY

Wear your mask when you go outdoors.
Wear your mask when you do your chores.
Wear your mask inside of stores.
Make sure you stay safe today.
Remember keep six feet away.

If you want to put my mind at ease,
There's one thing I ask you please.
Cover your mouth when you cough or sneeze.
Listen to what the experts say.
Please keep six feet away.

LAZY DOG

There once was a lazy old dog
Who liked to eat like a hog.
His greatest wish
Was to finish his dish
And then go to sleep like a log.

A BETTER TOMORROW

I wish for a day I could borrow
For today is so full of sorrow.
I'll lie down and rest
And hope for the best
And pray for a better tomorrow.

QUIET TIME

There are times when you want
To sit alone in silence
To ease your mind from stress and worry
And let the rest
Of the world go by.
Sometimes you just need to find
A quiet little corner
Away from the hustle and bustle
Without a worry or care.
There is nothing more comforting
Than to be at peace
In a place where you can rest
And meditate
And your tensions will start to cease.
Soon you will feel refreshed
And rejuvenated.
Then you can once again
Continue on your way.

TIME TO SAY GOODBYE

The time has come to say goodbye
To those we've come to know.
Although it's only been four years,
It seems so long ago.
The winds of change keep blowing.
That's a fact that we all know.
But we have no way of knowing
Which way the winds will blow.
We started out as strangers,
But soon our friendship grew.
So now with mixed emotions,
We bid a fond adieu.

SALLY IN THE VALLEY

I once know a girl named Sally.
We went for a walk in the valley.
I asked, "Pretty miss,
May I give you a kiss"?
She said, "Yes, but don't dilly dally."

NELLIE IN HER DELI

There once was a girl named Nellie
Who made sandwiches in her deli.
Ham and salami,
Bologna and pastrami,
But never peanut butter and jelly.

SAM AND EGGS

There once was a fellow named Sam,
Who liked to eat eggs and ham.
It was a nice treat
And to make it complete
He'd add toast with butter and jam.

In Memoriam

AGAINST ALL ODDS

Born in a small village in Italy in 1932 during the depression years
For Antonio Masullo, it was a time filled with doubt and fears.
To make matters worse, his father went to war and never came home
Leaving his mother to raise him and his sister alone.
The family lived through hard times with little to eat
But Antonio was determined not to succumb to defeat.
A trade he would need but which one to choose,
So, while still very young he learned to make shoes.
Soon he would marry and two children would he raise.
His love for them would last for all of his days.
In 1960 he left Italy for America by ship
It was a long and tedious trip.
Antonio left his mother, sister, wife and children in Italy
But two years later sent for his precious family.
Annuziata, Vincent and Rosanna arrived by plane
In 1962, they were united again.
He suffered many health issues, including TB.
But survived in spite of having only one kidney.
Through hard work and determination,
He raised a family in Brooklyn in his adopted nation.
His greatest pleasure was being with family
And eating authentic Italian food—a priority.
Vincent and Rosanna and their children were his pride.
The love he had for them cannot be denied.
Antonio lived through times both good and bad
And shared experiences happy and sad
But one thing for sure is true,
He accomplished all he intended to do.

DEDICATION TO MY MOTHER

After all those years on Earth
God has called you home.
You're reunited with those you love
So you won't be alone.
You left behind fond memories
Of good times that we had.
And although your passing
Has made us all feel sad,
We'll take comfort knowing
You're resting peacefully.
So until we meet again,
Please save a place for me.

IN MEMORY OF AUNT DOTTIE

You brought joy to everyone you met
That is why we never will forget
The way you always understood
And helped us any way you could.
You taught your children right from wrong
And encouraged them your whole life long.
Time cannot erase
The loving smile upon your face
Or the love you had for family
That will last eternally.
As we say our last goodbye
We'll feel the sorrow but will not cry
Knowing you're with God above
Where there is eternal peace and love.

DEDICATION TO MICHAEL

Michael was an easy-going guy
That's something no one can deny.
He always had a smile on his face
Any time and any place.
Michael was a patriot proud and true,
He served his country wearing Air Force blue.
Playing keyboard was his passion.
(Irish music never goes out of fashion).
While playing in a band, he met the love of his life.
Shortly, Carol became his wife.
They were married for many years,
Sharing joy and sorrow, laughter and tears.
But the person who meant the world to him
Was his pride and joy, his daughter Kim.
Michael faced many struggles, that's true
But the love of his family helped him through.
To everyone he was a true friend,
He was loyal right to the end.

Outdoors

THE SCENIC OVERLOOK

The sign read,
"SCENIC OVERLOOK CLOSED
FROM DUSK TO DAWN."
maybe they think there is nothing going on.
But as for me, I believe that they are wrong
to keep the scenic overlook closed from dusk to dawn.

I love to sit and watch the stars all twinkling bright
and look upon the moon as it shines its light.
I could gaze at the heaven all night long,
but the scenic overlook is closed from dusk to dawn.

Did you ever stop and listen to the sound
of crickets chirping all around
Or the nightingale singing its sweet song?
But the scenic overlook is closed from dusk to dawn.

It would be so wonderful if I could only stay
and watch the sunrise start a brand new day.
But I guess I'll have to move along,
because the scenic overlook is closed from dusk to dawn.

ON THE OTHER SIDE OF THE MOUNTAIN

On the other side of the mountain
is where I want to go,
where the breeze is always gentle
and the peaceful rivers flow.

Where the lake is azure blue
and the trees are ever green,
everyone seems so happy
worries are few and far between.

On the other side of the mountain
is the prettiest place I've ever seen.
the days are bright and sunny
and the nights are quiet and serene.

On the other side of the mountain
there's lots of wildlife.
all species live in harmony
everyone is free from strife.

People always greet you
with a smile and say hello.
on the other side of the mountain
is where I want to go.

A WALK IN THE PARK

I was a bright sunny day and so on a lark
I decided to take a stroll in the local park.
It was a pleasure to be out in the fresh clean air
And to admire nature everywhere.
In the open field, flowers were in bloom,
And the air was fragrant with their sweet perfume.
Up above I heard a sound coming from the trees.
I realized it was songbirds chirping melodies.
The sun was very warm, so I found a seat
On a bench in the shade to keep me from the heat.
Across the field some kids were playing ball.
It was the bottom of the ninth, the score tied, one all
With a runner on third base and just one out.
The batter swung and gave the ball a clout,
The runner crossed home plate with the winning run.
Win or lose, a baseball game is always lots of fun.
I got back up and continued on my walk,
Met an old friend, and we had a pleasant talk.
In the distance, I saw a young boy playing with a kite,
But it would not fly, try as he might.
The wind was too contrary, not blowing up but down.
He could not get the kite off of the ground.
Soon, it was time for me to leave the park,
As I wanted to get home before it got too dark.

YELLOW SNOW

While walking through the woods breathing crisp, clean air
Admiring the beauty that lies everywhere,
I remember what someone told me long ago,
"If you should get hungry, don't eat the yellow snow."
You can eat the berries growing on the trees,
Even eat the tree bark if you please.
But one thing you really ought to know
No matter how hungry you get, don't eat the yellow snow."
It's wonderful to walk and feel the frosty breeze,
Even though your body starts to freeze.
Just remember as you wander to and fro
No matter how tempted, don't eat the yellow snow.
I love walking through the fields of white,
Out here in the forest, it's such a pretty sight.
But soon it will be dark and the winds will start to blow
So, I'd better head back home before I eat the yellow snow.

A HOUSE ON A LAKE

I don't like water and I don't like to fish,
But to have a house on a lake is my greatest wish.
I don't have a kayak and I don't have a boat.
I don't know how to swim, why I can't even float.
But my one desire is to have a house out on a lake.
One day I'll get one no matter what it takes.
I'll get an easy chair and sit out on my dock.
Time will pass so quickly; I won't need a clock.
I'll go out in the morning to see the sun rise in the sky.
And look at the ducks all swimming and
birds flying way up high.
I'll sit on my dock all day with no worries on my mind.
That kind of peace is so very hard to find.
Later in the evening when the day is done,
I'll still be on the dock to watch the setting sun.
No, I don't like to sail or row and I don't like to fish,
But to have a house on a lake is my greatest wish.

RAIN

Here comes the rain again.
It's such a soothing sound
To hear drops falling down
Against my windowpane.

The gentle rain will help to grow my flowers,
With colors bright and scents so sweet.
I could sit and listen to the rain for hours.
A thick garden makes my life complete.

A short, light sprinkle is all I need
For my flowers to survive
And make my backyard come alive.
With the soil soft, I can plant some seeds.

THE SKUNK

Last week when I opened up my shed
What I smelled nearly stopped me dead.
It was an odor I knew well.
A wild skunk I did smell.
I didn't see him, and he didn't see me.
But I know he's out there. Where can he be?
Every night the scent grows stronger.
I can't take it any longer.
I'll get a trap and lay some bait.
That skunk will finally meet his fate.
So, I took the scraps from last night's meal,
Some chicken skin an orange peel.
I put them in the cage and set the lever.
Who knew I could be so clever?
The next morning right at sunrise
I went to the shed, but to my surprise
The food was gone without a trace
While the lever still remained in place.
That night I smelled the skunk again.
The odor was there despite the rain.
So, the next day I tried the trap once more.
This was becoming quite a chore.
Alas, the outcome was the same,
The skunk must think this is a game.
I thought I could out smart him, but I was wrong.
That skunk and I will learn to get along.

THE DEAD TREE IN MY YARD

Looking out my window, what did I see?
Right in the middle of my backyard
There was an old dead tree.
I'll go out and cut it down, that should not be hard.

I went into my shed and got an ax.
Everyone knows I'm cleaver.
So, I gave the tree several whacks,
But it stood as straight as ever.

Then I took out my tree saw.
I've used it many times before.
I cut and cut til my hand was raw,
And my muscles became quite sore.

After cutting for about an hour,
The tree fell to the ground
Just as I was running out of power.
It landed with a crashing sound.

Now you would think that's the end, my friend,
Since the tree has been chopped down.
But you'll have to think again,
'cause I can't leave it on the ground.

So, I proceeded to cut and chop some more,
Trying to cut the tree in two.
This is becoming quite a chore.
I'll be exhausted when I get through.

Finally, the tree was in pieces small,
And I placed them in a pile.
It was a tough job after all,
But a job well done makes me smile.

TWO PEACOCKS

A proud peacock with his head held high
Sees a cute peahen passing by.
He says to himself, "She looks so sweet,
There must be a way that we could meet."

So, he casually struts his stuff,
Hoping his colorful feathers are enough
To win the pretty peahen's love.
He holds his head high up above.

As he looks her in the eyes
He discovers to his surprise
The peahen wants no part of him.
His future with her has grown dim.

So, he slowly walks away
Hoping on some other day
Another peacock he'll chance to meet,
One who will make his life complete.

THE BLUEBIRDS OF HAPPINESS

The bluebirds of happiness are outside my windowsill.
Their presence is welcome after all that winter chill.
When the bluebirds of happiness begin to sing,
My heart is filled with joy, since that's a harbinger of spring.
The days are getting longer, the sun is shining bright,
And the bluebirds of happiness are such a lovely sight.
The bluebirds of happiness bring joy with their song.
My heart is filled with gladness and I want to sing along.
There are robins, sparrows, and the rest,
But the bluebirds of happiness are the very best.

GONE FISHING

I woke up to a sunny day and thought I'd have some fun.
So, I grabbed my bait and fishing pole
And went down to the fishing hole
To enjoy the summer sun.

When I got there no one was around.
Although the sun was blazing hot,
I found myself a shady spot,
Took out my rod and reel and sat down on the ground.

There were many fish, and they were biting well.
Every time I'd cast my line, the fish would bite.
A day like this is a fisherman's delight.
I would have a great day, I could tell.

I caught a lot of fish that day.
Some were big and some were small,
But the biggest one of all
Was the one that got away.

Holiday

NEW YEAR'S EVE TRADITIONS

Here are some New Year's Eve traditions
I learned when I was young.
They may sound kind of silly, but they were a lot of fun.

For dinner, always have beef or pork for luck
But never any chicken or duck.
The reason for this is a simple fact.
Cows and pigs walk forward, but poultry scratches back.

At midnight, blow whistles and bang pots and pans.
The first person in the house must be a dark-haired man.
He must walk around the house three times, then
enter through the front door.
When he gets inside the champagne begins to pour.
Everybody eats creamed herring (or pickled if you wish),
It doesn't matter as long as you have the fish.

Have money in your pocket, or you'll be broke all year long.
Keep it in a purse or locket, that way you can't go wrong.
Be on your best behavior if you know what's good for you.
Because what you do on New Year's Eve, you'll do the
whole year through.

VALENTINE'S DAY

Valentine's Day is here
And let me make it perfectly clear.
As time goes by, my love will not die
I'll love you each day of the year.

I'll give you a rose bouquet.
If you think that is okay.
I'll take you to dine with a bottle of wine
We'll have a wonderful day.

Perhaps if we get the chance
We could go out and dance.
The beat of a song could guide us along
And perhaps it will end in romance.

GROUNDHOG DAY

It's Groundhog Day when we find what the future brings,
Six more weeks of winter or an early spring.

The groundhog slowly leaves his comfy den
and looks up to the sky,
The sun is shining brightly right into his eyes.

He lowers his head and begins to look around
Suddenly he sees his shadow on the ground.

So, he shrugs his shoulders and walks back to his den,
For six more weeks he'll hibernate til spring comes back again.

But if the sky is dark and gloomy or clouds are in the air,
He does not see his shadow anywhere.

He stays outside and plays while we begin to sing,
Because that means we'll have an early spring.

ST. PATRICK'S DAY

It was St. Patrick's Day, so I thought I'd make the scene.
I took my lucky shamrock and pinned it to my shirt
of Kelly green.
There was a parade with floats and bands galore
To celebrate Patrick's arrival on the emerald shore.
The drum major led off and set the pace,
While bagpipers played, "Amazing Grace."
My friends and I waved as the Irish flag went by.
The orange, green, and white lifted our spirits high.
Afterward we went to our favorite pub
To partake of pints of ale and fine Irish grub,
Corned beef and cabbage, and my favorite, Shepherd's Pie.
Irish food is hardy, no one can deny.
When the band started playing our hearts were filled with joy,
But our eyes filled up with tears when we heard, "Danny Boy."
Watching the step dancers was a special treat.
They held their bodies rigid while they moved their feet.
St. Paddy's Day was a true delight.
A mug of Irish coffee was the perfect way to end the night.

THE TRUE MEANING OF EASTER

It's not about colored eggs or a chocolate candy bunny.
It's not about the flower bouquet that you gave your honey.
It isn't the basket filled with toys and jelly beans.
So, let me tell you what Easter really means.

Jesus was the Son of God, but some did not agree,
And so they decided to nail Him to a tree.
They placed thorns on His head and drove a
spear into His side,
Then laughed and mocked Him until He finally died.

His body was placed inside a borrowed tomb.
Those who believed in Him now were filled with gloom.
Early in the morning of the third day,
Some women came to roll the stone away.

But to their surprise an angel did appear.
He said, "The One you're looking for is no longer here.
Death could not hold Him, He is alive again,
Even as we speak, He walks with other men."

Yes, Jesus was God's Son, of that there is no doubt,
And that is what Easter is all about.

HALLOWEEN

Halloween season now is here,
when ghosts and goblins do appear.
It's such a fearful night,
as evil spirits start their flight.
If you venture out, beware.
There is danger lurking everywhere.
When the full moon starts to rise,
vampire bats fill the skies.
A wicked witch rides on her broom.
I see her silhouette across the moon.
In the distance, I hear a werewolf howl,
that can only mean he's on the prowl.
The sky is black except for a blood red moon,
which is a sign of gloom and doom.
A witch is at her cauldron casting up a spell.
This night is not going very well.
The cauldron is hot as an oven
(seven witches make a coven).
As a fierce wind starts to roar,
I hear a knocking on my door.
I open it up to find some beast
telling me, "It's trick or treat."
I give him some candy and close the door,
hoping he won't come back for more.
Halloween is called "Night of the Dead,"
a time of year I always dread.

THANKSGIVING

Thanksgiving Day will soon be here.
It brings joy our way,
With turkey to eat, parades to watch,
And football games to play.

As you gather with your family
Around the dining table,
Give thanks for those who came
And pray for those not able.

Some people travel far.
Others stay at home.
Some spend the day with friends.
Others are alone.

Whatever your lot in life
Whatever you possess,
Give thanks for what you have,
Remember someone else has less.

MARY'S BABY CHILD

On a cold December morn,
Mary's baby Child was born.
Among the cattle and the sheep,
She laid the Baby down to sleep.
In a manger she made His bed,
Then she knelt and bowed her head.
She said a prayer that He would be
The Savior who would set us free
From all our trials and our strife
And lead us to eternal life.

CHRISTMAS

C is for the Child born in a stable among the beasts.
H is for Heaven that shone so bright.
R is for the royals who came traveling from the East.
I is for incense, gold, and myrrh; gifts that were just right.
S is for shepherds who left their flocks at night.
T is for those who bowed their heads to pray.
M is for the manger where the Baby had lain.
A is for the angels who sang a joyous refrain
S is for the Savior who was born on Christmas Day.

Art & Poetry

The following section features Brenda's original abstract paintings accompanied by my poetic interpretation of those paintings.

This joint project came into being quite by accident. One day while Brenda was arranging her paintings for one of her art shows, I was inspired to write a poem about it. Brenda liked my poem so much that she included it with the painting at her exhibit. The combination of the poem and the related art received lots of positive responses, which led me to create poems for several of her other paintings. This special section features our collaborated efforts.

Enjoy the experience!

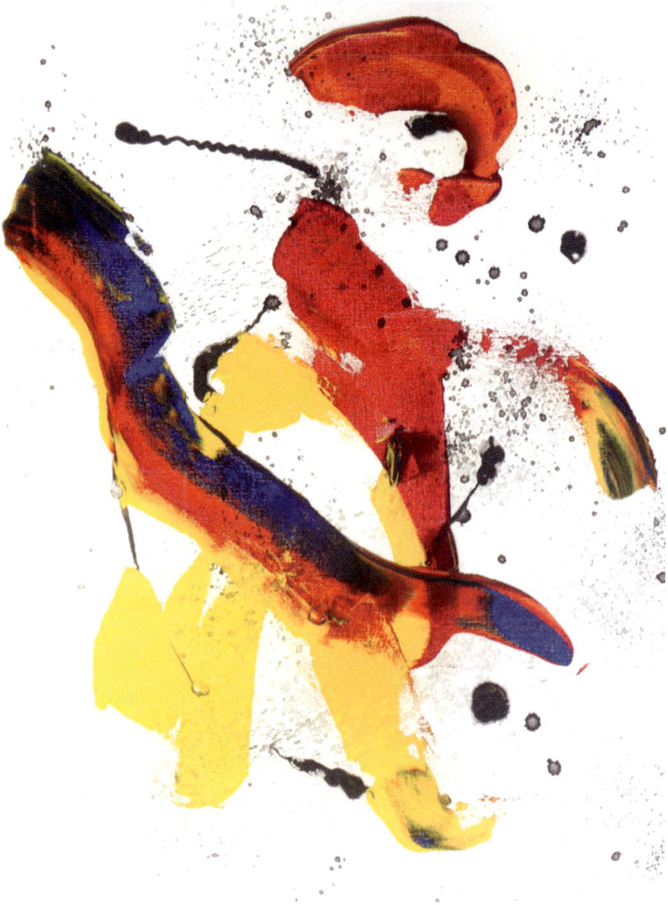

THE LADY WITH THE RED SHAWL

When the lady with the red shawl enters in the door,
All eyes are upon her as she glides across the floor.
As the lady in the red shawl walks across the room,
The men are all enchanted by the smell of her perfume.
She gives the men a smile as she passes by,
Looking like an angel with a twinkle in her eye.
No one ever saw the likes of her before,
Her very presence makes them crave for more.
The lady with the red shawl looks so elegant,
Everyone agrees, she must be heaven sent.
All the women are envious as they stare in awe
At the loveliest person that they ever saw.
There's no one else who can turn your head,
Like the lovely lady with the shawl of red.

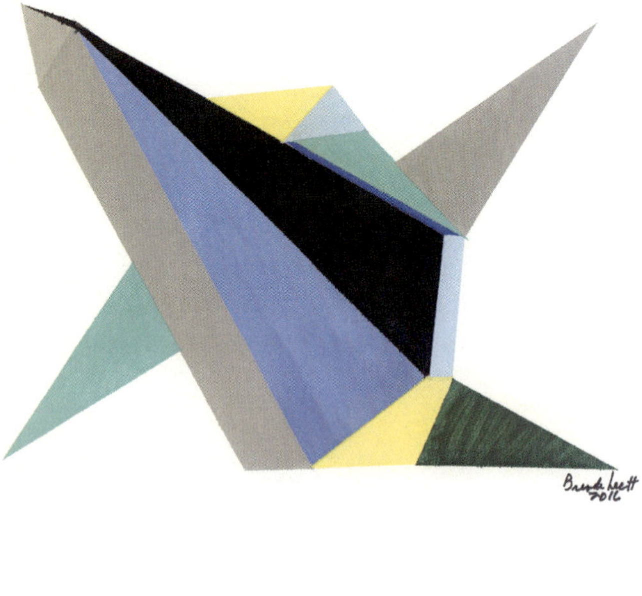

PYRAMID POWER

It is said that pyramids have strange powers
And can do miraculous things,
Like making sweet food that once was sour
Or change lead into golden rings.
They can make you feel just fine.
Some say they can change water into wine.
Pyramids can cure all of your ills
And warm you up if you have the chills.
If you're overweight, they can make you light as a feather,
Change old folks into young, or make you live forever.
Look into a pyramid to see what lies ahead
Or find a way to avoid what it is you dread.
A pyramid on your mantel can make your room serene,
One placed above your bed will give you pleasant dreams.
Put one in your garden to make the flowers grow.
A pyramid around your neck will set you all aglow.
A pyramid can do many things, whatever it is you choose.
So, go ahead and get one. What have you got to lose?
Pyramids can do wonders, that is plain to see.
But how they work remains a mystery.

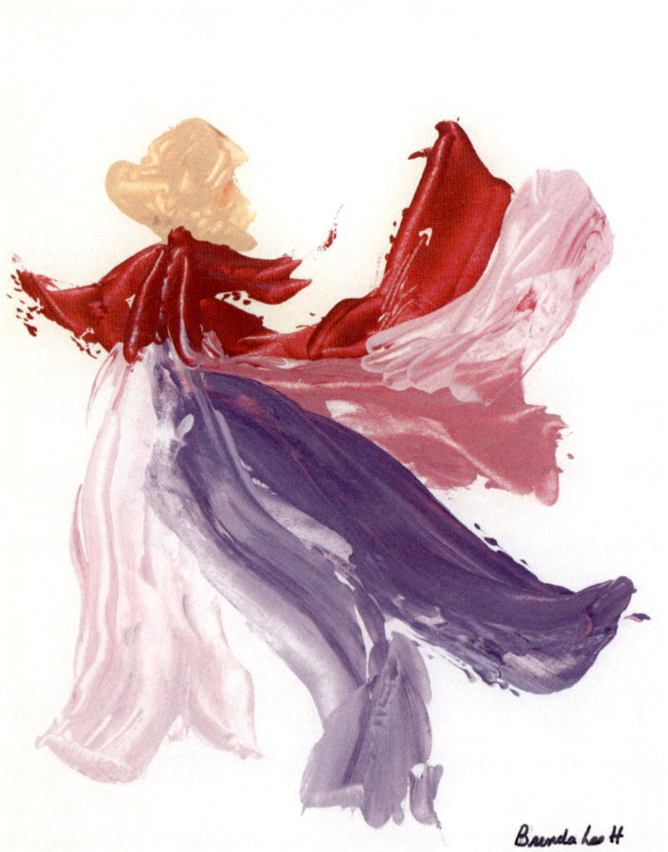
Brenda Lee H

CABARET DANCER

At the cabaret in gay Paree,
The dancers move so gracefully.
As they glide across the stage,
It's plain to see why they're the rage.
Listen to the music play, see them move their feet
As they dance and sway to the Parisienne beat.
If you want entertainment, listen to what I say,
Come to the cabaret.

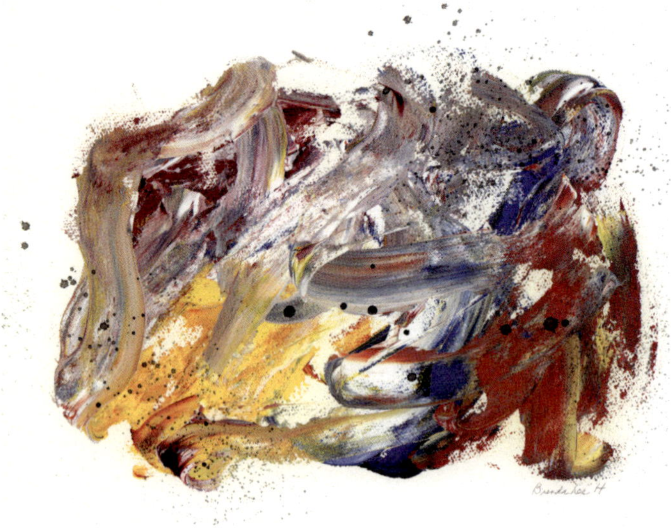

CHAOS

This world is filled with chaos and confusion,
Discontent and disillusion.
Simplicity is just and illusion.

Too many choices, too many ways
Complicate all of our days.
All this chaos is like living in a maze.

Chaos is all around,
calmness and reason cannot be found.
Disorder and insanity abound.

The world is getting more chaotic every day,
Everything seems to be in disarray.
Could it be that chaos is really here to stay?

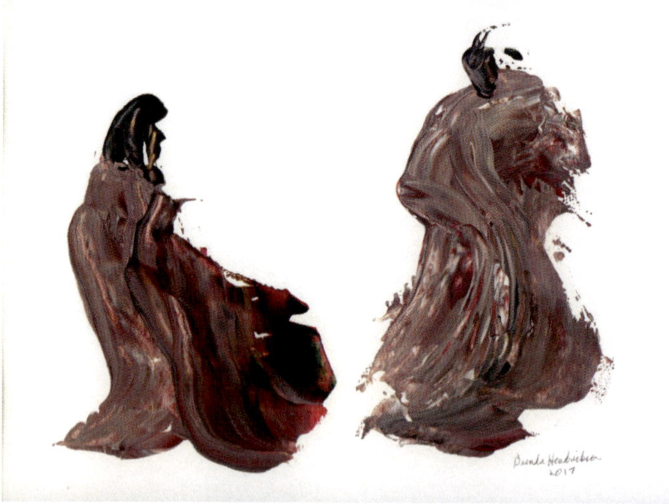

THE MEETING OF THE MINDS

The meeting of the minds is about to commence.
Was this meeting planned or just happenstance?
Will they unravel mysteries of the ages?
What words of wisdom will come from these sages?
Will they compare their philosophy
Or maybe discuss theology?
Perhaps they'll talk about science and math
Or how to walk down a righteous path,
Maybe how to maintain better health
Or ways to maximize one's wealth.
Will they discuss the state of the nation
Perhaps give their thoughts on creation?
Could they give their opinion on the economy
Or if Atlantis is on the bottom of the sea?
Will they speak of the causes of war and its aftermath
Maybe what causes hatred and wrath?
I wonder if they would discuss great works of art.
I wish they would discuss affairs of the heart.
Maybe we will never find out
What the meeting of the minds was about.

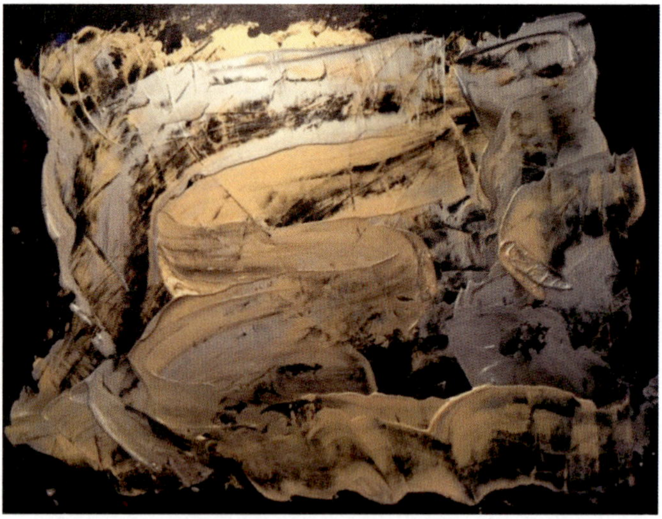

SILVER AND GOLD

Silver and gold are treasures.
Many say they measure wealth.
But riches aren't important.
What matters more is health.
So always remember to take care of yourself.
Silver and gold are precious.
That no one can deny.
But all the treasures you possess
Won't matter by and by.
For you can't take them with you when you die.
So, don't sit and worry about
How much you have in silver and gold.
What's more important in life
Is having someone to love and hold
Who will be beside you as you both grow old.

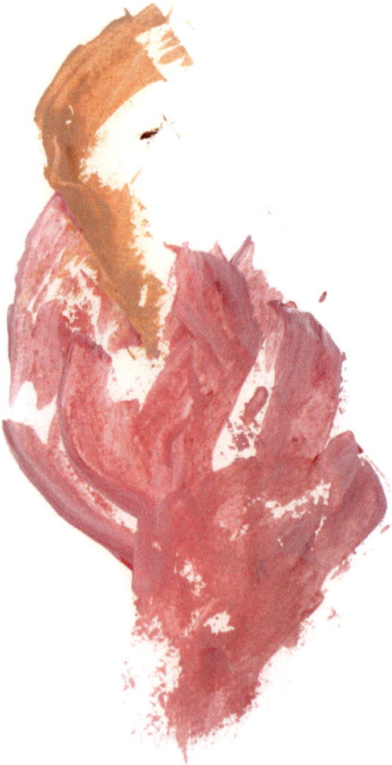

GEISHA HOSTESS

The geisha hostess of old Japan
Hides a smile behind her fan.
Her kimono is a vivid red,
While she wears a black wig on her head.
The tearoom is filled with music and song,
As the geisha dances all night long.
She moves about so gracefully,
And everybody will agree
She can entertain with ease.
The geisha hostess will aim to please.

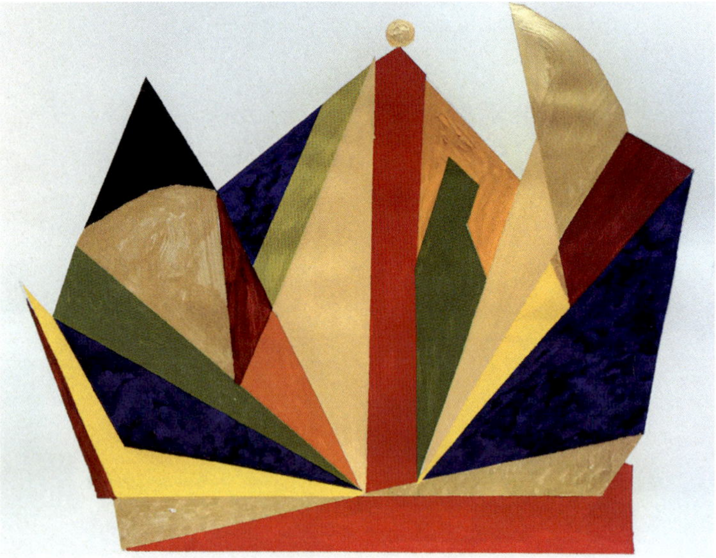

CROWN JEWELS

Crown jewels come in many hues,
Yellows, greens, reds, and blues.
Crown jewels are precious stones
With many styles and many tones.
Yellow garnet, blue sapphire,
Rubies bright red like fire,
Green emeralds stand out bold,
But most impressive are silver and gold.

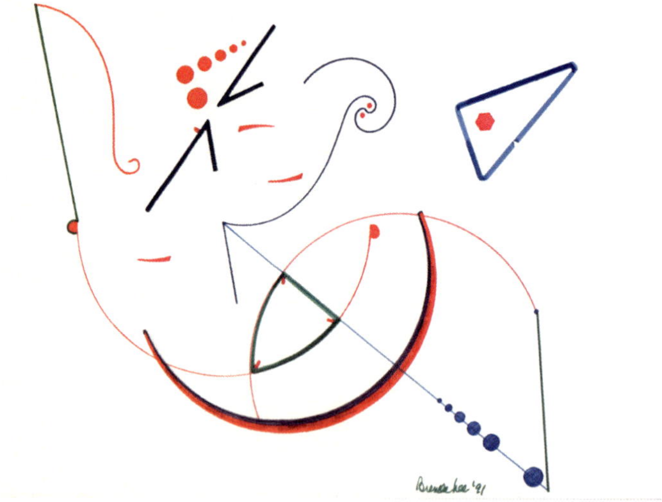

SMILING LADY

Smiling lady looking up at me.
Smiling lady lovely as can be.
Never have I seen a woman such as she
With style and grace that everyone can see.

Smiling lady sitting over there
With a face beyond compare.
All the men cannot help but stare
At her bright blue eyes and golden hair.

Smiling lady, may I take you home.
The hour is getting late, and I hate to be alone.
You look like a queen sitting on a throne.
How I'd love to have you for my own.

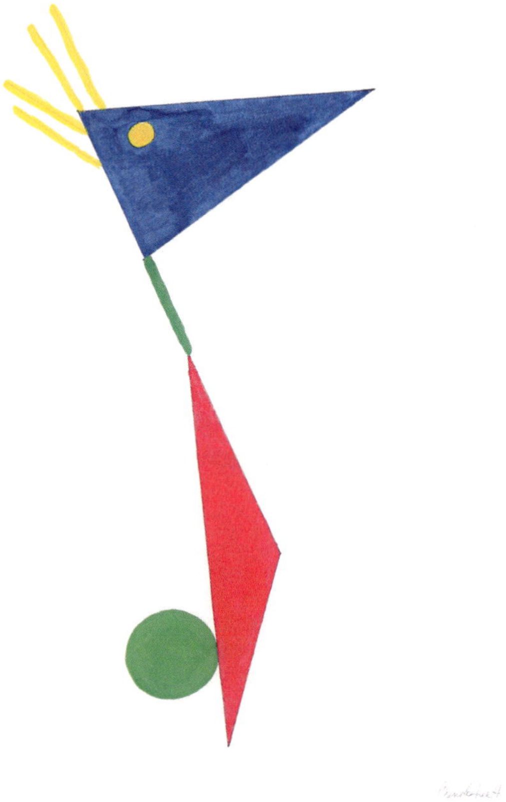

WOODPECKER

Woodpecker, woodpecker pecking on a tree,
Early in the morning disturbing me,
While I was sleeping peacefully.
Woodpecker, woodpecker, why can't you let me be?

Woodpecker, woodpecker on a limb,
I'm not sure if it's a her or a him.
All I know is it's pecking noisily.
Woodpecker, woodpecker, why can't you let me be?

Woodpecker, woodpecker outside my door
Keeps on pecking more and more.
The bird is pecking constantly.
Woodpecker, woodpecker, why can't you let me be?

Woodpecker, woodpecker on the tree
I can't see it but can it see me?
It keeps on pecking rapidly.
Woodpecker, woodpecker, why can't you let me be?

Woodpecker, woodpecker all day long,
Keeps on pecking loud and strong,
Putting little holes in my tree.
Woodpecker, woodpecker, why can't you let me be?

About the Author

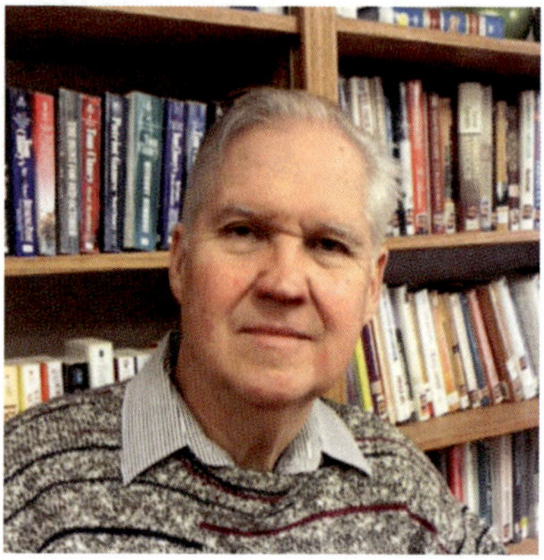

HOWARD HENDRICKSON

My first exposure to poetry was back in high school. As part of a creative writing class, we were required to compose different forms of literature, i.e., an essay, a one-act play, a short story, and poems. I found poetry to be the most interesting form because it allowed me to express myself, my thoughts, feelings, emotions, and fears more than any other forms of writing. Further classes in American and world literature in high school and college taught me to appreciate the great works of writers and poets.

Through the years, I dabbled with writing poems and song lyrics, which are closely related. However, I did not write seriously until several years ago when while surfing the Internet I stumbled upon an online poetry contest sponsored by The American Poetry Society. On a whim, I submitted a poem and to my surprise I was notified that the poem would be included in an anthology to be published later that year. A few months later, I received another letter asking for more poems to be submitted for inclusion in future volumes. That's when a lightning bolt hit me and I realized that they were making money off my poems and I wasn't receiving any royalties. I decide to publish my own book, thus my poetry career took off. I have since had three books published and numerous book signings and readings with a following on my Facebook group, "Fans of Howard's Poetry." As a published author, it has given me the opportunity to do a number of commissioned works (e.g., a poem for a published golfing book) and special events. I hope this latest book gains the same positive response as my previous endeavors.

About the Artist

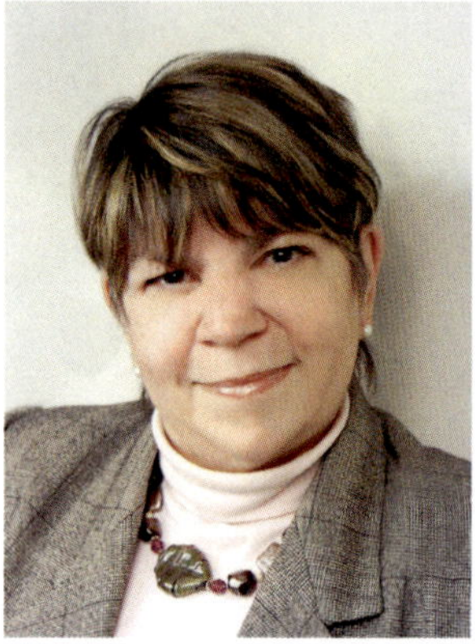

BRENDA HENDRICKSON

A lover of the arts since growing up in Manhattan, New York, I was fortunate to live within walking distance to the Metropolitan Museum of Art, a short bus ride to major galleries, and a subway ride to SOHO or the Village. My style has been abstract art since the early 1990s, with inspiration by masters such as Miro, Kantinsky, Mondrian, Picasso, and Tarkay.

I am an award-winning businesswoman, author, as well as an abstract artist. What do technical and artistic qualities have in common, you ask? They both engage the individual to make judgments both analytically and emotionally. I start with a line, shape, or color. The palette knife is my tool of choice. It affords me the freedom of mixing colors right on canvass or paper. Acrylics dry fast, so that other layers of paint can be added to enhance painting. Then, I name the piece according to what it represents, maybe a flower, an animal, a person, or a symbol.

Abstract artists are not limited to realism. We use our intuition, inspiration, and imagination skills to create an image for the viewer's mind's eye. We encourage mental exercises, and there is no right or wrong of the viewer's interpretation. Our creations are visual challenges that we as artists encourage—What do you see?

I have exhibited at many galleries (Studio Montclair, ACL, Morris County Library, and Koehler) had some one-woman shows (Kearney Bank, Parsippany Library). My paintings hang in many in private collections, and I am studying at The Art Students League. I am a member of the West Essex Art Association and Studio Montclair. My signature piece is *The Lady with the Red Shawl*, using the palette knife technique.

The Published Books of Howard Hendrickson

Dreams, Thoughts, and Memories

Life, Love, and Laughter

My World, My Words

Available at Amazon.com and BarnesandNoble.com

Visit "Fans of Howard's Poetry" on Facebook